Table of Contents

"Leadership is solving problems. The day soldiers stop bringing you their problems is the day you have stopped leading them. They have either lost confidence that you can help or concluded you do not care. Either case is a failure of leadership."[1]

-General Colin Powell

Introduction

The primary focus of this paper is to understand the implications of leader development through mentorship if the Army adds an additional maneuver battalion to the existing force structure of the Brigade Combat Team. The goal of the research is to understand the possible degradation of quality time Brigade Combat Team commanders are able to spend with subordinate commanders during the critical professional development period of company command, and the role their mentorship can play in the overall development of these commanders into the strategic leaders of the future.

In 1999, then Chief of Staff of the Army, General Eric Shinseki, plotted a course for transforming the Army that has dramatically changed the way it is organized and fights. The brigade centric formation that now makes up the Army is the result of years of thought, war gaming, and careful programming throughout the budgetary process. The Army embarked on this transformation agenda focused on future threats the United States could face. The Army White Paper published in 2001, described a world with adaptive enemies who would meet the United States asymmetrically. Just a few months after the publishing of the transformation

---

[1] Military Connection, http://www.militaryconnection.com/military-quotes/colin-powell.asp (accessed December 8, 2011)

1

campaign plan the authors were proven correct in their forward thinking of how a new enemy would attack the U.S. on September the 11th, 2001.

> "The world is changing and so too are our adversaries. At one end of the spectrum, creative and adaptive opponents will employ strategies to destroy U.S. resolve by attacking our homeland, our culture, exploit our vulnerabilities, and seek to fracture confidence in public institutions, generate economic uncertainty, and divide the focus as well as the will of the general public."[2]

The new Brigade Combat Team formation has proven to be very lethal in both Iraq and Afghanistan during the last 9 years of combat in the Global War on Terrorism.

The pre-transformation brigade was made up of three organic maneuver battalions augmented by the parent division with various enabler formations depending on the threat and operating environment. The new transformed Brigade Combat Team would lose one full maneuver battalion but gain an organic fires battalion (artillery), forward support battalion for logistics, Brigade Special Troops Battalion, and a cavalry squadron for reconnaissance. This change has made the Brigade Combat Team and its six organic battalions the centerpiece of the Army's formations and has given the brigade commander unparalleled options when employing this formation.[3]

The reason for moving forward with the transformation plan was hard learned lessons during the prelude to operations in both the Persian Gulf in 1990 and the Balkans in 1999. In each of these operations, the Army was criticized for being too slow when deploying forces oversees. Then Chief of Staff of the Army, General Eric Shinseki announced:

---

[2] Headquarters, U.S. Department of the Army, *United States Army White Paper: Concepts for the Objective Force,* (Washington, D.C. June 2001), 2.

[3] Headquarters, U.S. Department of the Army, *Field Manual 3-90.6: Brigade Combat Team,* (Washington, DC, September 2010), 1-6.

"Our heavy forces are too heavy and our light forces lack staying power. Heavy forces must be more strategically deployable and more agile with a smaller logistical footprint, and light forces must be more lethal, survivable, and tactically mobile. Achieving this paradigm will require innovative thinking about structure, modernization efforts, and spending."[4]

There are three basic types of Brigade Combat Teams. These BCTs are the Infantry Brigade Combat Team (IBCT) (Appendix 1), the Heavy Brigade Combat Team (HBCT) (Appendix 2), and the Stryker Brigade Combat Team (SBCT) (Appendix 3). Each of these formations has their own unique characteristics, mainly the equipment they employ, be it tanks, Stryker combat vehicles, or the Infantryman. They all, however, are built around approximately

The changes in the Brigade Combat Team modified table of organizational equipment (MTOE) have not come without some criticism. Early in Iraq there were many division commanders as well as brigade commanders who were frustrated over the lack of combat troop strength in these new formations. It was clear that the Brigade Combat Team, while larger than the pre-modular formation, lacked the operational reach due to the loss of the third maneuver battalion and the addition of the reconnaissance squadron. The Brigade Combat Team, while growing overall in personnel strength, lost one maneuver company post reorganization.[5] The loss of the maneuver company does not seem that big until it is compounded by the number of Brigade Combat Teams in the Army. The pre-modular force, known as the Army of Excellence (Active, National Guard, and Reserve), had 233 combat battalions with 699 maneuver companies at the end of fiscal year 2004. By the end of 2011, Army plans called for 161 maneuver

---

[4] Benjamen S. Lambeth, "Task Force Hawk," Air *Force Magazine (*February 2002): 83.

[5] Congress of the United States, *Options for Restructuring the Army* (Washington D.C. Congressional Budget Office, May 2005), 69.

battalions with 541 maneuver companies-roughly a thirty percent drop in the number of battalions and a twenty two percent drop in the number of companies.[6]

The counter to the loss of the maneuver company is the overall deployability and survivability of this formation. In previous conflicts, one spoke of forward-deployed Army divisions; the focus in Afghanistan and Iraq is on deployed Brigade Combat Teams. The goal of transformation was to enable the brigade to deploy independently of the parent division. To this end, modular force brigades have major combat support and service support capabilities organic to their structure.[7] This paradigm shift has enabled the Army, with the Brigade Combat Team (BCT) as its core formation, to be an expeditionary force.

Another criticism of the brigade combat team formation is the lack of senior leader mentorship for the low density military occupational specialties (MOS) within the brigade. The current trend for selecting Brigade Combat Team commanders is from the pool of officers who have successfully commanded maneuver battalions. This in turn means that the experience brigade commanders currently have is focused on two out of the six battalion formations in the brigade. Pre-modular brigades would be solely made up of the maneuver battalions and the enablers that the brigade would receive for operations would come from the parent division. The artillery, logistical, communication, and engineer expertise came from organizations that the division commander owned. These formations had commanders of their own, who in turn provided the mentorship and guidance to junior officers in their career growth. With the shift to the modular formation of the Brigade Combat Team, this expertise and senior level mentorship

---

[6] Andrew F. Krepinevich, *Strategy for the Long Haul: An Army at the Crossroads* (Washington D.C. Center for Strategic and Budgetary Assessments, 2008), 14

[7] Ibid., 13.

has been lost for the non-maneuver elements within the brigade. Career progression and subsequent command billets have been radically reduced for these military occupational specialties in the overall effort to transform the Army into the modular Brigade Combat Team formation and an expeditionary force.

The strategic landscape that forces in the future will be required to fight and win the nation's wars is ever changing and dynamic. Chief of Staff of the Army, General George Casey and Secretary of the Army, John McHugh stated in the 2011 Army Posture Statement,

> "The war is not over yet; we still face a ruthless foe. We remain in an era of persistent conflict. In order to prepare for an uncertain future and an increasingly complex strategic environment we must maintain the combat edge gained during the last decade of war, reconstitute the force and continue to build resilience into our formations and people. These efforts will ensure that we continue to prevail in the fights we are in today and are prepared for new challenges in the future."[8]

In order to grow adaptive and strategic leaders and to maintain the quality leadership within the Army's officer corps, mentorship will continue to have an enormous impact on junior officer development. In their work published in *Military Review*, authors LTG Bagnal, LTC's Eric Pence and Thomas Meriwether describe the importance of developing leaders: "The development of leaders who can fight and win on the future battlefield is perhaps the greatest challenge facing the Army today. The challenge in educating and training the leaders of tomorrow is to provide them with the capability to be flexible-to innovate, think and adapt to the demands of a fast-paced, highly stressful, rapidly changing environment."[9] To accomplish this education, senior leaders within the Brigade Combat Team will have to understand the

---

[8] Headquarters, U.S. Department of the Army, *At a Strategic Crossroads: 2011 Army Posture Statement,* (Washington, D.C. March 2011), 1.

[9] Charles W. Bagnal, Earle C. Pence, and Thomas N. Meriwether, "Leaders as Mentors," *Military Review* (July 1985): 6.

importance of mentorship and time management when grooming junior officers for positions of increasing responsibility, regardless of the differences in the commanders and the junior officer's specialty.

The Army has been focused on mentorship numerous times throughout its history. In 1985, Chief of Staff of the Army, General John A. Wickham Jr. stressed the importance of mentorship in his White Paper designating that year "The Year of Leadership."[10] That same year General Wickham directed a study to determine the need for a formal mentoring program within the Army and also on the overall officer professional development program out to the year 2025. Results of the study suggested that senior leaders understood the importance of senior leader involvement with subordinate officer professional development. In the survey, "95 percent of the General Officers surveyed felt the professional development of subordinates was just as much a leader's responsibility as accomplishing the mission."[11] Mentorship is a critical tool in the overall effort in officer professional development.

Mentorship as a leader development tool has many different elements to it to be successful but one of the most critical is time. Commanders must make an investment in time with subordinate leaders in order to successfully mentor them for growth not only as leaders within the Brigade Combat Team but as future strategic leaders for the Army and the Nation as a whole. In the 2011 Posture Statement, the Army's leaders stressed the importance of leader development when they stated, "The Army will continue its commitment to leader, individual,

---

[10] Ibid., 14.

[11] Nate Hunsinger, "Mentorship: Growing Company Grade Officers," *Military Review,* (September-October 2004): 82.

and collective training in order to remain mentally, physically, and emotionally agile against a highly decentralized and adaptive foe."[12]

An agile force is one that can quickly act on mission type orders from higher headquarters. The importance of understanding intent within orders from higher command is currently stressed in numerous Field Manuals in the Army's doctrine. This understanding is grounded in historical experiences. General Friedrich W. Von Mellenthin, Chief of Staff of the 5th Panzer Army in World War II stated, "To follow a command or an order requires that it is also thought through on the level from which the order was given. The follow through requires that the person to whom it was given thinks at least one level above the one at which that order was given."[13]

The conditions from which General Von Mellenthin describes have only become more important on today's highly complex, decentralized, and non-linear battlefield. Educating junior officers to be successful in this environment will be one of the most important functions of the brigade commander. Whether it is professionally developing the logistics company commander on supplying the brigade during operations or the infantry company commander on the importance of synchronizing fire support assets when maneuvering, mentorship will continue to be an important tool for the brigade commander's use. These junior officers will face an environment very close to the one that General Shinseki described eleven years ago when he stated; "The quality, maturity, experience, and intellectual development of Army leaders and

---

[12] Headquarters, U.S. Department of the Army, *At a Strategic Crossroads: 2011 Army Posture Statement* (Washington, D.C. March 2011), 6.

[13] Charles W. Bagnal, Earle C. Pence, and Thomas N. Meriwether, "Leaders as Mentors," *Military Review* (July 1985): 5.

Soldiers become even more critical in handling the broader range of simultaneous missions in this complex operational environment."[14]

The same year the Army embarked on the transformation campaign plan a disturbing report was released addressing the reasons behind the alarming attrition rate of captains and majors in the Army. The 2001 Army Training and Leader Development Panel led by Lieutenant General William Steele described an environment where junior officers felt disconnected with their commanders and a general lack of confidence between the two groups. Additionally, the panel discovered that there was a general perception of zero tolerance for mistakes as well as a general feeling that communication with senior leaders was nonexistent with regard to the junior officer's career development.[15] The attacks of 11 September 2001 and the subsequent operational pace that the Army has encountered over the last nine years have placed these concerns in the background as the War on Terror was prosecuted. These concerns are starting to surface once again, however, now that the Army has ended operations in Iraq, and potentially, in Afghanistan. In the 5 December 2011 edition of the *Army Times* junior leaders voiced their concerns over the amount of "face time" they currently have with senior leaders and the importance the junior officer places on the time senior officers are willing to give to them through mentorship.[16] The number one complaint of the junior officers who were interviewed was the amount of quality time they had with their senior leaders. One solder reported, "Our major weapon system is the

---

[14] Headquarters, U.S. Department of the Army, *United States Army White Paper: Concepts for the Objective Force,* (Washington, D.C. June 2001), 2.

[15] William M. Steele, LTG, "Training and developing Army Leaders," *Military Review* (July-August 2001): 6. http://www.au.af.mil/au/awc/awcgate/milreview/steele.pdf (accessed November 2011)

[16] Michael Tan, "Staying Tough on Standards," *Army Times* (December 5, 2011)

soldier, and we need to spend a little more time on the human dimension in our PME."[17] Again, time is the most important element in the mentorship tool kit.

The current budgetary constraint on the Department of Defense only exacerbates the increasing concern over long term officer professional development in this era of persistent conflict. Looming budget shortfalls could lead to certain reductions in force structure as well as manning of the force. Concern has been raised over how to conduct this force reduction without losing the resiliency of the combat tested officer corps. One of the proposals in the current debate on how to reduce the overall Brigade Combat Team numbers in the Army is to cross level maneuver battalions from deactivating brigades in order to give each Brigade Combat Team an additional maneuver battalion or in essence increasing the size of the remaining brigades to seven organic battalions. This proposal has picked up steam because it addresses the criticism of senior leaders who feel there are not enough soldiers in the current organization of Brigade Combat Teams when employed in a counter insurgency fight, in which the nation is currently involved. This lack of maneuver troop strength was one of the top concerns in a report to congress by the Center for Strategic and Budgetary Assessments in 2008 in which the authors stated, "The loss of ground maneuver capability- boots on the ground-seems at odds with the services ongoing irregular warfare operations, which are often manpower-intensive."[18] The addition of the third maneuver battalion to the already existing six battalions seems to address these concerns.

The current operating environment in Afghanistan places increased responsibilities at the lowest levels on the battlefield. Platoon leaders and company commanders are operating at

---

[17] Ibid.

[18] Andrew F. Krepinevich, *Strategy for the Long Haul: An Army at the Crossroads* (Washington D.C. Center for Strategic and Budgetary Assessments, 2008), 14.

increasing distances from their battalion and brigade commander's locations. They are making decisions that have far reaching strategic impacts during fast paced engagements. It can be argued that their education and professional development is more important today than it ever has been in history. History also informs that this will not be the last conflict the Unites States is faced with and enemies learn from the success and failures of those who fought the Army in the past. Armed with this knowledge, the responsibility for this professional development rests on the shoulders of the brigade commander who is the senior leader of the formation around which the Army has formed. Lieutenant Colonel Harry Ingram wrote in an article on leader behavior in units, "You coach one level below but mentor two levels down. That means colonels mentor captains, lieutenant colonels mentor lieutenants, and first sergeants and captains mentor squad leaders."[19] He continues describing why it is important that organizations utilize mentorship not only to build trust between leaders but for the importance of understanding why the higher headquarters is asking the subordinate unit to accomplish a mission. He states, "The purpose of mentoring is to provide the junior with a glimpse of the context in which the superior makes decisions. This is crucial if, as our doctrine proposes, leaders at all levels grasp and implement the intent of those two levels removed."[20]

Adding a maneuver battalion could have an adverse effect on the long term professional development of the junior officers within the Brigade Combat Team. The high operational pace of the Brigade Combat Team, coupled with the increased span of control placed on the brigade commander who now employs six organic battalions, could be strained more with an additional

---

[19] Larry H. Ingraham, "Caring is Not Enough: An Uninvited Talk to Army Leaders," *Military Review* (December 1987): 47.

[20] Ibid.

10

maneuver battalion made up of four companies. The commander will have to stretch the most important element in leader development, time, to meet the new demands on the enhanced brigade.

Historical examples of the professional development of strategic leaders in the Army's past give a glimpse to the importance mentorship had on their careers and professional growth. Leaders like General's Dwight D. Eisenhower, Douglas MacArthur, and Omar N. Bradley all provided important lessons learned in how they grew to become the preeminent leaders of their generation. Names like General's George C. Marshall, Fox Conner, and John Pershing have all had a dramatic impact on the generation that followed them in the Army. Their mentorship model, however, needs to be understood in today's contemporary operating environment in order to understand the importance this leadership development tool has on the education of the future leaders for the Army and the Nation.

Again, the primary focus of this paper is to understand the implications of leader development through mentorship if the Army adds an additional maneuver battalion to the existing force structure of the Brigade Combat Team. The goal of the research is to understand the possible degradation of quality time Brigade Combat Team commanders are able to spend with subordinate commanders during the critical professional development period of company command and the role their mentorship can play in the overall development of these commanders into the strategic leaders of the future.

Part one of this study will focus on historical military leaders and the impact mentorship had on their professional development. Part two will focus on the organization of the Brigade Combat Team and future design proposals. The amount of time senior commanders can spend with subordinate commanders due to the size of the Brigade Combat Team will be examined in this section as well. Part three will focus on current leader development models and how mentorship fits into office professional development. Finally, part four will analyze the

11

implications of growing the Brigade Combat Team with an additional battalion on leader development through mentorship and a recommendation derived from these findings.

"Before you are a leader, success is all about growing yourself. When you become a leader, success is all about growing others."[21]

-Jack Welch

Lessons from History

History is filled with examples of strategic leaders and the impact they have had on the battlefield. Their professional development throughout incredibly successful careers can provide a template on how strategic leaders are formed with the help of mentors in their lives. Generals Marshall, Bradley, Eisenhower and Patton all had a major impact on the outcome of World War II. These strategic leaders progressed through the ranks in the interwar years with the help of key mentors in their lives. Their mentors spent countless time and energy on professionally developing these officers in order that they would become strategic leaders of the future. Analyzing the time spent with the mentors will provide insight into the importance of the mentorship relationship in officer professional development.

The career progressions of these officers do not fit into the current Army officer development model. These officers spent years with mentors learning their craft. The most important lesson from these examples is the amount of time invested by senior leaders on the individual growth of the junior officer. In today's Army, it is the brigade commander who is charged with assessing the future potential of junior officers during the critical development billet

---

[21] Mentor Quotes, http://www.self-improvement-mentor.com/famous-leadership-quotes.html (Accessed 29 December, 2011) Jack Welch is the retired CEO of General Electric who is credited with increasing the company's wealth 4000 percent during his tenure.

of company command. The lessons of mentorship from Generals like Eisenhower, Bradley, and Marshall point to how critical these assessments are for the future of the Army and nation.

General Dwight D. Eisenhower

General Eisenhower met one of his most influential mentors at a dinner party hosted by General Patton in Washington D.C. At the time, both Patton and Eisenhower had a similar interest in the future use of tanks on the battlefield. General Patton invited General Pershing's Chief of Staff, Fox Conner, over for the dinner party. There, Eisenhower impressed Conner with his knowledge of tanks and his thoughts on employing them in combat. Conner, a few short months later, had Eisenhower assigned as his executive officer in the Panama Canal Zone at Camp Gaillard where Conner was a Brigade Commander. Eisenhower served in this capacity from January 1922 until September 1924.

General Eisenhower has called the years assigned with Fox Conner the most interesting and constructive years of his life. [22] Major General Conner, then a Brigadier General, saw the potential in Eisenhower and spent countless time and energy preparing the young officer for increasing levels of responsibility that would come with future promotions. General Eisenhower did not see himself as a student of military affairs. He said about himself, "I did not think of myself as either a scholar whose position would depend on the knowledge he had acquired in school or as a military figure whose professional career might be seriously affected by his academic or disciplinary record."[23]

---

[22] Cole C. Kingseed, "Mentoring General Ike," *Military Review* (October 1990): 26-30.

[23] Dwight D. Eisenhower, *At Ease: Stories I Tell to Friends* (Garden City, New York: Doubleday and Company, 1967): 12

14

Once he discovered that General Eisenhower did not like studying military history, BG Conner set out to train Eisenhower on works by important military authors[24]. He read books by Jomini and Clausewitz, and studied the exploits of Fredrick the Great. General Eisenhower describes countless hours spent with Fox Conner analyzing battles ranging from the Napoleon Wars to the United States Civil War. BG Conner would assign the reading of each battle and after Eisenhower completed the reading they would engage in why the leaders of the battles made the decisions they did. They would often engage in this dialogue while horseback riding in the Canal Zone.

BG Conner and Eisenhower also discussed lessons learned from World War I where Conner served as the operations officer for General Pershing. BG Conner was convinced a war would again erupt in Europe due to the shortcomings of the Treaty of Versailles. He articulated to Eisenhower how a unified allied command would have to be created this time in order to keep short term national interest from interfering with the long term strategic objectives of winning the war.[25] These discussions had a huge impact on Eisenhower in the years to come in World War II.

The mentorship relationship did not stop once Eisenhower was reassigned away from the tutelage of then BG Conner. MG Conner continued to groom Eisenhower from a distance. Knowing how important Command and General Staff College (CGSC) attendance was for an up and coming officer, MG Conner arranged to have Eisenhower assigned out of the infantry in order to secure a spot in the school out of the Adjutant Generals allotment. He did this without Eisenhower's knowledge. He instructed him through telegrams to be patient and not argue with

---

[24] Cole C. Kingseed, "Mentoring General Ike," *Military Review* (October 1990): 26-30.

[25] Lawrence F. Camacho, *The Leadership Development of Dwight D. Eisenhower and George S Patton JR.* (Fort Leavenworth, School of Advanced Military Studies, 2009): 27.

orders from the War Department.[26]   The lessons in Panama in military history, operations order

preparation, and terrain management under the careful eye of BG Conner prepared Eisenhower to

succeed at CGSC and ultimately graduate at the top of his class.

Eisenhower continued to utilize the advice and counsel from his mentor throughout his

career. MG Conner assisted him with assignments and recommendations on where and with

whom to serve with as he progressed in his profession. Later in his career when he was selected

as Commanding General, Europeans Theater of Operations, General Eisenhower wrote to MG

Conner, "I cannot tell you how much I would appreciate at this moment, an opportunity for an

hour's discussion with you…".[27]

The importance of the mentorship relationship between MG Fox Conner and General

Eisenhower would be manifested years later before the death of Eisenhower. He wrote in a

personal memoir, "I can never adequately express my gratitude to this one gentleman, for it took

me years before I fully realized the value of what he had led me through. But in a lifetime of

association with great and good men, he is the one more or less invisible figure to whom I owe an

incalculable debt."[28]

General Omar N. Bradley

One of the most important relationships in General Bradley's career was one with

General George Marshall. General Bradley worked for General Marshall when he was a

---

[26] Ibid., 28.

[27] Cole C. Kingseed, "Mentoring General Ike," *Military Review* (October 1990): 26-30.

[28] Dwight D. Eisenhower, *At Ease: Stories I Tell to Friends* (Garden City, New York: Doubleday and Company, 1967): 187

lieutenant colonel at the Infantry School at Fort Benning. General Marshall selected Bradley to

lead the Weapons Section at the school. General Bradley learned Marshall's leadership style and

excelled in that environment where he received little guidance about the position. Marshall

placed him in position and expected him to perform and, because of his freedom of latitude, to

excel.[29]

General Marshall continued to provide advice and mentorship to General Bradley

following their posting to Fort Benning. General Bradley followed General Marshall to the

General Staff where he had the duty of reading important documents and preparing one page

analysis of them for Marshall. Here General Bradley learned the inner workings of higher

commands. General Bradley continued to impress his mentor and was soon recommended by

him to assume the position of Assistant Commandant of the Infantry School. This position was a

brigadier general's billet and Bradley was promoted to that rank from lieutenant colonel. Clearly,

the relationship established with Marshall was one of the most important for General Bradley's

professional development. General Bradley later wrote of this relationship by stating, "No man

had a greater influence on me personally or professionally."[30] General Marshall's ability to

judge, correctly, officer's potential was validated in the career accomplishments of General

Bradley, who rose to five stars and held the position of General of the Army.

General George C. Marshall

General Marshall learned from multiple mentors throughout his career and became

arguably one of the most influential leaders and mentors in the United States Army's history.

---

[29] Joseph C. Dooley, *George C. Marshall: A Study in Mentorship* (Carlisle Barracks, PA: U.S. Army War College, 1990), 14.

[30]Omar N. Bradley and Clay Blair, *A General's Life* (New York: Simon and Schuster, 1983), 63.

General Marshall served as aide de camp to three influential Army Generals. He was Aide de camp first to General Hunter Liggett in 1915 and then General Franklin Bell in 1916. Following these two assignments, General Marshall was picked by General Pershing, whose position at the time was the equivalent to today's Chief of Staff of the Army, to be his aide de camp. General Marshall held this position for 5 years with General Pershing and it was one of the most influential assignments of his career.

Serving as Aide de Camp, culminating with his relationship with General Pershing, General Marshall learned the inner workings of high level command and the political aspects of these assignments in Washington D.C. General Marshall was able to watch as the senior officer in the Army went about his duties on a daily basis and his interactions, not only with Army officers serving under him, but also with Congress and the President of the United States. General Marshall said of his assignment with General Pershing when writing him years later, "My five years with you will always remain the unique experience of my career..."[31]

The most important lesson that General Marshall took from his experiences on these senior staffs was an understanding of leader development and the importance of mentoring subordinate officers for positions of increasing responsibility. General Pershing's efforts with General Marshall set up the latter to be a highly successful leader of the Army during World War II. In essence, General Pershing trained his successor, albeit one who would hold the position years later during a critical time in the nation's history.

General Marshall's keen eye for talent enabled him to pick the majority of officers who would later serve as general officers in World War II. An estimated 160 officers who

---

[31] Forrest C. Poque, *George C. Marshall: Education of a General 1880-1939* (New York: The Viking Press, 1963): 226.

worked at Fort Benning during Marshall's tenure as the Assistant Commandant of the Infantry School became general officers in World War II.[32] According to his wife, General Marshall never forgot a brilliant performance or one that was bad.[33] His uncanny ability to recognize talent for future service became legendary within the Army as it was widely rumored that he kept a book of officer's names with whom he had observed at Benning and in future travels. In this book, he reportedly would annotate the officer's potential and would update the record following future engagements with the officers.

The officers that General Marshall mentored during the interwar years became some of the most celebrated leaders of World War II. General Omar Bradley was chosen to be Chief of Weapons Section, a while later General Joseph Stillwell was assigned as the head of the Tactics Department.[34] Additionally, General Eisenhower worked closely with General Marshall, under the advisement of his mentor General Fox Conner, were he served as the Chief of Operations Division in the War Department. General Eisenhower's relationship with General Marshall would grow from this assignment to the latter recommending Eisenhower first to command in Europe and then to succeed him upon his retirement.

General George Patton

General Patton strived to be the best in every assignment he was given and this internal drive gained him the attention of superiors who mentored him throughout his career. His first company commander, Captain Francis C. Marshall (later Brigadier General), quickly noted

---

[32] G. Joseph Kopser, "Mentoring in the Military: Not Everybody Gets It," *Military Review* (November-December 2002): 40.

[33] Joseph C. Dooley, *George C. Marshall: A Study in Mentorship* (Carlisle Barracks, PA:U.S. Army War College, 1990), 13.

[34] Ibid., 14.

that Patton was an excellent officer with unlimited potential. He assisted Lieutenant Patton with a future assignment to Fort Meyer, Virginia where his abilities would be noted by the senior leaders in the Army who lived there. It was here that Patton quickly made a name for himself on the small influential post as an expert polo player and earned a spot on the Olympic team in the Pentathlon. [35]

One of the most important relationships from his posting at Fort Meyer was with Secretary of War, Henry Stimson. The two met while horseback riding on the post and soon became friends. The Secretary had Patton act as his aide at important social events, assisting in Patton's name recognition among the senior military officers and political leaders of the time. Patton also earned the admiration of then Chief of Staff of the Army, General Leonard Wood and soon was reassigned to his office. His new duties to both General Wood and Secretary of War Stimson, required his attendance at various activities as well as being the action officer in the headquarters. His position helped him gain an appreciation of everyday activities within the Army's highest staff. These lessons would become critical in the overall development of General Patton when he would achieve command of high level organizations[36].

General Patton's next crucial mentorship relationship was with General Pershing during his expeditions against Pancho Villa in Mexico. Patton convinced Pershing to take him along on the expedition as an additional aide de camp. Patton gained fame during the expedition by utilizing vehicles in combat for the first time in United States Army history as well as killing

---

[35] Carlo D'Este, *Patton: A Genius for War* (New York: HarperCollins Publishing, 1995), 128-139.
[36] Ibid.

one of Pancho Villa's main corroborators as well as capturing another.[37] General Pershing was impressed with Lieutenant Patton's performance and when selected to organize and lead a division in World War I, General Pershing personally requested, in writing, Patton's assignment to his staff as the adjutant[38]. The lessons from this posting helped him understand the intricacies of leading men and maneuvering in combat, a skill that he would master for World War II. Patton was soon transferred from this posting and promoted because of the high marks he received from Pershing but more importantly his mentor was preparing him for service at the next higher position.

General Pershing was selected to lead the First Army in combat and he sent, once again, for mentee Patton to join him, this time as a tank brigade commander. General Patton's unit performed very well in various engagements and he was awarded the Distinguished Service Medal for his actions in World War I.

The professional development of these four strategic leaders from the past depicts the importance that senior officer guidance was to their overall success. The knowledge they gained through hours of professional mentorship proved invaluable to them as they rose in rank. These lessons are important to understand in order to build strategic leaders now for the Army and the Nation.

---

[37] Lawrence F. Camacho, *The Leadership Development of Dwight D. Eisenhower and George S Patton JR* (Fort Leavenworth, School of Advanced Military Studies, 2009): 69.

[38] Carlo D'Este, Patton: *A Genius for War* (New York: HarperCollins Publishing, 1995), 191.

"You go to war with the Army you have, not the Army you might want or wish to have at a later time." [39]

- Secretary of Defense Donald Rumsfeld.

Brigade Combat Team Organization

The Army radically altered the existing structure of the brigade in order to make a unit that was highly deployable and self sustaining. The pre-transformation organization known as the Army of Excellence, with its three organic maneuver battalions, was designed to fight and win in Europe with an existing logistical structure in place. According to military strategist BG Huba Wass de Czege, "The Army was designed primarily to defeat a numerically superior mechanized threat backed by strong air and naval forces, on territory of an ally, and from a forward-deployed posture in which essential ground support and sustainment infrastructure already was in place."[40] This opportunity to test the effectiveness of this formation came to fruition with the overwhelming tactical victory in Desert Storm. The division-based Army overwhelmingly destroyed the numerically superior forces of Saddam Hussein, reinforcing the belief of the effectiveness of this formation. Future adversaries, however, used the lessons of Desert Storm in attempts to defeat the large formations of the US Army by engaging them in urban or inhospitable terrain. No adversary would want to fight the US Army in open terrain in the near future.

The turbulent political landscape of the 1990's brought the Army to realize that it had to transform its formations in order to stay relevant in this new era. The nation faced sending forces overseas to counter new asymmetric threats in places like Somalia, Rwanda, Haiti, and Bosnia. These missions had threats that were unlike those faced in Desert Storm and often were more

---

[39] Donald Rumsfeld, *Known and Unknown: A Memoir* (New York: Penguin books, 2011), 645.

[40] Huba Wass de Czege and Richard Hart Sinnreich, *Conceptual Foundations of a Transformed US Army* (Washington, DC: Institute for Land Warfare, March 2002), 9.

focused on peacekeeping than war fighting. These new hot spots also had the problem of austere infrastructures that posed a problem for the division-centric formations. The difficulty deploying the Army to these locations, coupled with the desire to keep a smaller footprint while there, led Army leaders to transform the Army to an expeditionary force that could sustain itself while in theatre. This new formation would be named the Modular Force.

Led by then CSA General Eric Shinseki, the Army transformed its brigade combat teams into the modular force with the hope that emergent technologies would enable the brigades to "see first, understand first, act first and finish decisively."[41] Additionally, the Brigades would be deployed for longer periods of time without their parent division structure supporting them. This led the Army to build the new modular force with increased combat support and combat service support structure than it would normally receive from the division when deployed to combat.

The attacks of 11 September 2001 made it necessary to deploy large numbers of soldiers overseas to fight both in Iraq and Afghanistan for an extended period of time. This requirement led the Army to continue its transformation initiative while fighting in both of these countries. Army leaders instituted Army Force Generation (ARFORGEN, Appendix 6) as a means to manage the deployment of forces to both Iraq and Afghanistan over an extended period of time. ARFORGEN, focused mainly on brigade size formations, gave senior leaders flexibility when planning what units would deploy for rotations in combat and when they would go. This flexibility also provided leaders with a tool to provide some resilience into the total force while maintaining a large footprint in both Iraq and Afghanistan.

---

[41] Headquarters, U.S. Department of the Army, *United States Army White Paper: Concepts for the Objective Force* (Washington, D.C. June 2001), iv.

The modular force unit now known as the Brigade Combat Team (BCT) is much larger than the old formation in sheer numbers of soldiers. The main growth, however, was in the combat support and combat service support battalions added to the force structure. The actual numbers of infantry, in the IBCT, actually decreased with the elimination of one maneuver battalion. The original designers of this formation thought the decrease in one maneuver battalion would be offset with the creation of the reconnaissance battalion, which in theory, would enable the BCT to see the enemy first, thus making the BCT more lethal than the brigade of pre-transformation design.

The old brigade had on average thirteen company commanders within the brigade. This position, arguably, is the most critical for professional development in a young officer's career. A company commander is responsible for everything his unit does or fails to do. According to FM 6-22 *Army Leadership*, "Command is about sacred trust. Nowhere else do superiors have to answer for how their subordinates live and act beyond duty hours. Society and the Army look to commanders to ensure that Soldiers and Army civilians receive the proper training and care, uphold expected values, and accomplish assigned missions."[42] The responsibility placed at the foot of these young officers, some with as little as four years of service under their belts, is enormous.

The company commander is not alone in determining the road he or she will take while in command. They receive direction and guidance from the battalion commander and the brigade commander in carrying out their duties as company commanders. It is the relationship with the brigade commander that is extremely important to the young company commanders. The brigade

---

[42] Headquarters, U.S. Department of the Army, *FM 6-22 Army Leadership: Competent, Confident, and Agile* (Washington, D.C. 12 October 2006), 2-3.

commander is the senior rater in the evaluation system for the company commander. He or she also is the senior leader in the brigade and provides the overall direction, command climate, and example for the brigade's leaders to follow. The brigade commander is also the best suited to provide career counsel and mentorship to the young company commanders under their charge. FM 6-22 describes the importance of developing subordinate leaders in this manner, "The leader must invest adequate time and effort to develop individual subordinates and build effective teams. Success demands a fine balance of teaching, counseling, coaching, and mentoring."[43]

The increase in size of the Brigade Combat Team has brought with it numerous advantages over the old formation, as well as some disadvantages. The sheer number of company commanders that are now under the brigade umbrella is a major difference in the two formations. The new BCT has on average thirty companies assigned to it. Each of these company commanders is looking for guidance and mentorship from the senior commander in the BCT. The BCT commander, however, has time as his or her biggest constraint in providing adequate mentorship to these company commanders.

The Army defines mentorship as the voluntary developmental relationship that exists between a person of greater experience and a person of lesser experience that is characterized by mutual trust and respect.[44] The brigade commander is in a critical leadership position that has long lasting effects on leadership for the young company commanders as they look to model their behavior off of a successful leader within their chain of command. This critical relationship between the company commanders and their brigade commander has become even more

---

[43] Headquarters, U.S. Department of the Army, *FM 6-22 Army Leadership: Competent, Confident, and Agile* (Washington, D.C. 12 October 2006), 8-1.

[44] Headquarters, U.S. Department of the Army, Army *Mentorship Handbook* (Washington, D.C. January 2005), 4.

important over the last ten years that the Army has been engaged in sustained combat operations in both Afghanistan and Iraq. The decentralized nature of this conflict has made it even more important for young commanders, who at times operate very far from the brigade and battalion commanders' location, to have someone with whom they can model their leadership attributes after. According to FM 3-24, the Army's Counterinsurgency manual, "Combat in counterinsurgency is frequently a small-unit leader's fight; however, commanders' actions at brigade and division levels can be more significant. Senior leaders set the conditions and the tone for all actions by subordinates."[45]

The current pace of operations, due to the sustained combat operations, has placed a strain on the amount of time senior commanders within the BCT have with subordinate commanders during training and operations overseas. BCT commanders are charged with ensuring their unit is prepared for answering the nation's call. While at home station, there is a myriad of tasks that must be accomplished in order to ensure success on the battlefield. Numerous leader intensive exercises are needed to ensure the commanders at the company level are fully prepared to lead their companies in combat. Exercises such as indirect fire support control, live fires, platoon through company level maneuvers, and air to ground coordination, all require the expertise of the BCT commander to certify his subordinate commanders. These requirements, along with professional development schools, mandatory post deployment leave, and permanent change of station orders for key leaders all shorten the amount of time BCT commanders have to train their subordinate commanders. These difficulties are stressed even

---

[45] Headquarters, U.S. Department of the Army, *FM 3-24 Counterinsurgency* (Washington, D.C. December 2006), 7-1.

more when the amount of company commanders within the brigade is increased into the training pool.

The BCT formation also has another impediment built into it in terms of leader development. The majority of company commanders within a BCT are not from the combat arms (Infantry, Armor, and Artillery). As stated earlier, the greatest change between the Total Army brigade and the BCT is the increase in combat support and combat service support structure. These companies are being led by young captains who now do not have a senior commander of their same branch as their brigade commander. In the division-centric Army, these leaders would have been assigned to a Division Logistics command (DISCOM), Engineer Brigade, or a Division Artillery Brigade (DIVARTY), for example. They would have had senior leaders of the same branch who had the same experiences that the company commander has to mentor them through the company command professional development block. This is all now done by the maneuver BCT commander who is also certifying these leaders in their critical task for combat operations.

The current budgetary issues with the federal government have the potential to threaten the long- term professional development of the officer corps if not closely monitored by senior Army leaders. Due to the high national debt, the Army, along with the rest of the services, has been directed in recent months to downsize their overall end strength.[46] According to Chief of

---

[46] Tom Vanden Brook, "Defense Secretary Leon Panetta defends a leaner military," *USA Today* (January 1, 2012), HTTP://www.usatoday.com/news/washington/story/2012-01-26/panetta-military-defense-cuts/52805056/1 (accessed 12 March 2012).

Staff of the Army General Odierno, one of the ways the Army will look to reduce its overall end strength is to reduce the number of BCTs in the active and reserve components.[47]

At the same time Army leaders look to trim force structure, they also are looking at addressing the perceived shortcomings of the BCT. A proposal that has gained momentum is to trim the overall number of BCTs out of the Army inventory and at the same time add a maneuver battalion to the remaining BCTs. This would address the shortage of boots on the ground that has been echoed by numerous division commanders in Iraq and Afghanistan when discussing the shortcomings of the current BCT organization. The Congressional Research Service noted, "The reduction in ground maneuver capability-often referred to as "presence" or "boots on the ground"- may adversely impact the BCT's ability to conduct counterinsurgency operation which often require the ability to cover large areas with a sufficient number of soldiers to provide security and to defeat and deter insurgents."[48]

The addition of a maneuver battalion to the BCT would add to its overall lethality, especially in the current operations in Afghanistan. The additional boots on the ground potentially means the BCT can hold more terrain or train additional numbers of host nation forces. It also could create more time at home station within the ARFORGEN model due to the need for less BCTs in Afghanistan to conduct operations.[49]

One of the negative aspects in adding another maneuver battalion to the existing force structure of the BCT, however, is the amount of time company commanders within the BCT

---

[47] Carlo Munoz, "Army Eyes Deeper Brigade Combat Team Cuts, Odierno Says," *AoL Defense.* (24 February 2012), HTTP://www.defemse.aol.com/2012/02/24/army-eyes-deeper-brigade-combat-team-cuts-odierno-says (accessed 12 March 2012).

[48] Andrew Feickert, *U.S. Army's Modular Redesign: Issues for Congress* (Washington D.C. Congressional Research Service, Library of Congress 5 May, 20068) 14.

[49] Lance M. Bacon, "Army to Lose another 5 BCTs," *Army Times* (March 5, 2012)

would have with their senior rater, the BCT commander. An already stretched command would absorb an additional six company commanders and their teams into a time-constrained professional development environment. Over the long term, the effects on professional development of strategic leaders of the future might be seriously impeded due to the shortened amount of time senior leaders within the BCT can spend with these young commanders during this critical, impressionable time.

"If your actions inspire others to dream more, learn more, do more and become more, you are a leader.[50]

- John Quincy Adams

Leader Development in the Army

One of the core missions of the Army is to provide trained and equipped forces prepared to answer the nation's call whenever and wherever needed. According to CSA General Schoomaker, "The Army's core competencies are to train and equip soldiers and grow leaders and to provide relevant and ready land power capability to the combatant commander as part of the joint team."[51] The most important factor in these missions is preparing leaders to face the challenges of the 21st century. FM 22-100 *Army Leadership* states, "Leadership is influencing people—by providing purpose, direction, and motivation—while operating to accomplish the mission and improving the organization."[52]

There are many tools available to the Army in preparing leaders for increasing levels of responsibility. The Army has numerous professional development schools that sequentially build over the lifetime of an officer to prepare them for each rank they hold. An example of this would be the Officer Basic Course, attended as a new lieutenant, followed by the Career Course when the officer reaches captain and then Intermediate Level Schooling once the officer reaches the rank of major. Each of these professional development schools provides the student with the

---

[50] Mentor Quotes, http://www.self-improvement-mentor.com/famous-leadership-quotes.html (Accessed 29 December, 2011)

[51] General Peter Schoomaker and Major Anthony Vassalo, "The Way Ahead," *Military Review* (March-April 2004): 5.

[52] Headquarters, U.S. Department of the Army, *FM 22-100 Army Leadership: Be, Know, Do* (Washington, D.C. August 1999), 1-4.

tools he or she will need to be successful in the functions they will be required to perform in a unit once graduated from the course. Additionally, the soldier will learn enormously from on-the-job execution of task under the watchful eye of senior leaders within the unit, as well as at training events overseen by observers and controllers. Arguably the most important learning will take place at the unit where, paired with a senior non-commissioned officer, the junior leader learns the skills and attributes that will make them successful over the course of their career.

The Army Training and Leader Development Model (Appendix 4) depicts the areas that a leader is professionally developed over their lifetime. There are three separate but overlapping areas, operational, institutional and self-development, that when synchronized, achieve the goal of a trained soldier.[53] The main avenue, through which the Army does this, is training. According to Army Regulation 350-1, "Training builds confidence and competence, while providing essential skills and knowledge. Leader development is the deliberate, continuous, sequential, and progressive process - grounded in Army values - that develop Soldiers and Army civilians into competent and confident leaders capable of decisive action, mission accomplishment, and taking care of Soldiers and their Families."[54]

In essence, a leader becomes one through training and senior leader involvement in their professional development. CSA General Gordon Sullivan put it this way when stressing the importance of leader involvement in subordinate leader development, "Developing your subordinates is your legacy to the future. They do not have to be born to be leaders-they can be

---

[53] Headquarters, U.S. Department of the Army, *AR 350-1 Army Training and Leader Development* (Washington, D.C. December 2009), 4.

[54] Ibid.

31

developed. You do this by putting your arm around them, or kicking them in the ass, whichever is needed."[55]

Senior leaders have to create an environment where developing future leaders for the long term health of the organization, the Army, is as important as mission accomplishment is in the near term. Authors Noel Tichy and Eli Cohen suggest in their book, *The Leadership Engine*,

> "Winning organizations win because they have good leaders who nurture the development of other leaders at all levels of the organization….the ultimate test for a leader is not whether he or she makes smart decisions and takes decisive action, but whether he or she teaches others to be leaders and builds an organization that can sustain its success even when he or she is not around."[56]

It is a good leader who sets up an atmosphere of nurturing the growth of the organizations future leaders. This is the true legacy of a good leader.

The Army Training and Leader Development Panel (ATLDP) in 2000 found many junior grade officers very dissatisfied with the overall training they received through the then-current education model. They believed the career model they were under, which focused on preparing leaders to face a conventional threat, did not fit into the professional development needs of the current force and the potential adversaries they would face. They also did not feel they were being mentored by a senior officer corps that was more and more distant from their subordinate commanders, creating a culture of micromanagement, a perceived zero defect culture, and a feeling of non-committal from senior officers to their subordinates.[57] The study provided many recommendations to senior Army leaders, many of which were immediately instituted such as

---

[55] Major Mark D. Rocke and Major Thomas W. Hayden, "Officer Development: A Doctrinal Imperative," *Military Review* (January 1993): 29.

[56] Noel Tichy and Eli Cohen, *The Leadership Engine: How Winning Companies Build Leaders at Every Level* (New York, New York: Harper Collins Publishing, 1997),

[57] Lieutenant General William M. Steele and Lieutenant Colonel Robert P. Walters, "Training and Developing Army Leaders," *Military Review* (July-August 2001): 4.

universal Command and General Staff College attendance (now termed Intermediate Level Education or ILE) and increased opportunities for Joint Professional Education. Young officers also voiced their opinion that the Army needed to provide more opportunities for broadening assignments outside of the field focused Army. Advanced civil schooling, opportunities with industry, and exposure to government and high level Army and Joint Staff positions were all perceived as valuable professional development assignments to the officers surveyed in the study. An increase in the total number of allocated slots available for each of these broadening assignments was a direct result of the panel's findings.

The attacks of 11 September 2001 overshadowed the changes instituted in the ATLDP by the increased operational tempo and requirements placed on the Army. As the U.S. enters the final stages of the Iraq War and with decreasing commitments in Afghanistan, the Army will once more need to analyze the study's findings in order not to have to relearn the same lessons. In the end, the same type of leaders that were needed before the wars started will be required to lead the Army further into the 21st century. The Secretary of the Army discussed this new leader in a speech to the ILE class of 2005,

> "In short, Army leaders in this century need to be pentathletes, multi-skilled leaders who can thrive in uncertain and complex operating environments... innovative and adaptive leaders who are expert in the art and science of the profession of arms. The Army needs leaders who are decisive, innovative, adaptive, culturally astute, effective communicators and dedicated to life-long learning."[58]

In the fiscal year 10-11 Army Training and Leader Development Guidance, CSA General George Casey again reiterated the need to refocus efforts on professional development and

---

[58] Headquarters, U.S. Department of the Army, *FM 6-22 Army Leadership: Competent, Confident, and Agile* (Washington, D.C. 12 October 2006), 7-1.

education in order to prepare our junior leaders for the stresses of leadership in an era of persistent conflict.[59]

Leader involvement in subordinate leader development will always remain a critical element in producing capable leaders for the future of the Army and mentorship is one of the most beneficial tools for the senior commander. In his article, 'Mentoring in the Military: Not everybody gets it', Josepth Kopser states, "Mentoring is far more than just teaching or coaching. Mentoring is about trust, friendship, and in the end, wisdom."[60] Mentoring is a way to address the perceived gulf that exists between the senior commander and the junior officer, annotated in the ATLDP 2000 study, therefore building trust throughout the ranks. According to Major General Lon Maggart, who wrote on the importance of mentorship in leader development, "Personal mentorship between senior and junior leaders is essential in filling information gaps, and mentorship provides another avenue to help motivate, educate and guide quality people to higher levels of performance and responsibility.[61]

Kathy Kram, who has written extensively on the effects of mentorship in the workplace, describes in her book, _Mentoring at Work: Developmental Relationships in Organizational Life_, the differences in mentoring roles and functions. A mentor performs two functions during a relationship: career functions and psychological functions. Career functions are those that enhance career development and psychological functions are those that enhance the sense of

---

[59] General George W. Casey Jr, _Army Training and Leader Development Guidance FY10-11_ (Washington, D.C. 31 July 2009), 5.

[60] Josepth Kopser, "Mentoring in the Military: Not Everybody Gets It," _Military Review_ (November-December 2002): 40.

[61] Lon Maggart, "Mentoring-A Critical Element in Leader Development," _Military Review_ (May-June 1999): 86.

competence, identity and effectiveness in a professional role.[62]   Mentoring is a time consuming

effort and one into which, due to the shortened timeline within units, not all officers will have the

opportunity to enter.

The Army describes the importance of mentoring as a development tool in every Field

Manual on leadership. There is a web link on Army Knowledge Online that is dedicated to

helping junior officers and senior officers enter into a mentorship relationship. This site will aid

officers in determining what kind of mentor they are seeking and also what to expect out of the

relationship. There are also numerous articles from the Army's medical establishment on the

importance of mentoring in the development of quality leaders. The CSA, General Peter

Schoomaker, called 2005 the "year of leaving a legacy through mentorship".[63]   Through this

program headed by the office of the Deputy Chief of Staff for Personnel, the Army created the

Army Mentorship Handbook. This resource aids leaders on what mentoring entails, the stages

each team will go through, and gives resources available to both the mentor and the mentee.[64]

Even with all of the importance placed on mentoring in the development of leaders in the

Army, there is no real forcing function to ensure that mentoring is happening in units. The idea

of making mentoring mandatory for senior and subordinate leaders is not new but has never fully

been codified. CSA General Wickham challenged all leaders to become mentors as a result of the

leadership study he commissioned in 1985.[65]   Chief of Staff's Schoomaker and Casey have both

---

[62] Kathy E Kram, *Mentoring at Work: Developmental Relationships in Organizational Life* (Boston, MA: University Press of America, 1988), 23.

[63] Headquarters, U.S. Department of the Army, *Army Mentorship Handbook* (Washington, D.C. January 2005), 3.

[64] Ibid.

[65] Charles W. Bagnal, Earle C. Pence, and Thomas N. Meriwether, "Leaders as Mentors," *Military Review* (July 1985): 6.

called on leaders in the Army to step up and be mentors but fell short of saying it was a required practice. The reason the practice has yet to be made mandatory is because mentoring is a time consuming effort.[66]

The amount of time brigade commanders and company commanders have together in a BCT is very short. Usually a command tour for a BCT commander is two years in length, depending on where the unit is in the ARFORGEN cycle on assumption of command. The company commanders can expect anywhere from eighteen to twenty four months of command time, arguably the most important position they can hold for developmental purposes. These times can be shortened or lengthened based on many variables in an officer's career; professional schooling, second commands, broadening assignment opportunity, and aide de camp openings are but a few. Each of these assignments can be very beneficial to a young officer but inadvertently shorten the amount of time young officers have in a BCT where they learn important leadership skills from non-commissioned officers and their senior commanders.

Army manuals stress the importance of creating a climate of learning and development within an organization for it to be effective. FM 6-22 *Army Leadership* provides the characteristics of successful organizational climates as including include a clear, widely known purpose, well-trained and confident soldiers, disciplined, cohesive teams, and trusted, competent leaders.[67] The leaders of these organizations also have the overall responsibility of developing their subordinate leaders for increasing levels of responsibility through a multitude of resources to include realistic training, on-the-job learning, and professional mentorship by senior leaders.

---

[66] Kathy E Kram, *Mentoring at Work: Developmental Relationships in Organizational Life* (Boston, MA: University Press of America, 1988), 19.

[67] Headquarters, U.S. Department of the Army, *FM 6-22 Army Leadership: Competent, Confident, and Agile* (Washington, D.C. 12 October 2006), 11-5.

According to FM 6-22 Army Leadership, "Operational leaders know they bear major responsibility for training the leadership of tomorrow's Army."[68] Additionally, the Army describes eight core competencies that individuals must possess to be effective leaders and the majority of them are the ability to develop others (Appendix 5). These core competencies include; leads others, extends influence beyond the chain of command, leads by example, communicates, creates a positive environment, prepares self, develops others, and gets results.

CSA General Casey laid out his plan for unit and leader development in his guidance issued for all general officers, senior executive service, and their Command Sergeants Majors in the summer of 2009. This guidance stressed the need to take advantage of the increased dwell time in units gained from the drawdown in Iraq and a focus on training units and developing leaders. His guidance told commanders to focus training in units on these necessary training task: Officer Education System, Non-Commissioned Officer Education System, physical training, critical functional training, new equipment training, individual training and qualification, crew and team training/certification, comprehensive soldier fitness, family reintegration, battle staff training, post-deployment health screening, and property accountability.[69] This training is focused on the basics for a unit when building a cohesive team of teams.

General Casey also stressed the importance of leader development in this era of persistent conflict. He stated that commanders needed to invest time and energy to grow the next generation of leaders through an appropriate balance of education, training, and experiences.[70] Commanders were responsible for this by creating a climate that would encourage self

---

[68] Ibid.

[69] General George W. Casey Jr, *Army Training and Leader Development Guidance FY10-11* (Washington, D.C. 31 July 2009), 4.

[70] Ibid., 5.

development and lifelong learning. He also stressed the importance that commanders encourage subordinate leaders to seek opportunities that would broaden their professional education. Opportunities like graduate school, teaching, training with industry, assignments to governmental agencies, and training and advising indigenous partners were all given as examples of professional development that should be looked as career enhancing. These opportunities would in the end broaden an officer's view on geopolitical pressures and an understanding of the environment in which they will operate throughout the duration of their careers.

Another way the Army develops leaders in units is through the joint combat training centers. Each of these centers provides realistic training for every level of leadership within a BCT. The lessons learned at these combat training centers have been born out in Afghanistan and Iraq with incredible results. These training centers are one of the best tools for the BCT commander to use in preparing their unit for combat operations but also in assessing subordinate leader abilities in an environment that most closely resembles what will be faced in a real world scenario. The ability for the BCT commander to create an atmosphere that replicates what a combat training center can at home station is very limited due to the lack of resources and time available.[71]

The definition of success for leader development in the Army for the majority of officers is increasing levels of command assignments. It appears over time that the pools of officers that are selected for BCT command come directly from officers who commanded a maneuver

---

[71] Headquarters, U.S. Department of the Army, *2010 U.S. Army Posture Statement* (Washington, D.C. 1 December 2009) HTTPS://secureweb2.hqda.pentagon.mil/vdas_armyposturestatement/2010/information_papers_combate_training_center_CTC_program.asp (Accessed 20 March 2012)

battalion in a BCT successfully in the past.[72] These officers were selected to command a

maneuver battalion based on the success they had as a company commander within a BCT and

their performance as a major in a key and developmental position in a battalion or BCT, such as

operations officer or executive officer. Statistics from the last few battalion command selection

list suggest that the time officers spend in key positions within a BCT like company command are

crucial to their overall opportunity for selection to increasing levels of command in the future. [73]

The key person in the assessment of these officers is, and will continue to be in the future, the

BCT commander, who is responsible for the training, professional development, and assessment

of the overall effectiveness of these junior officers within their BCT.

One of the issues facing the overall development of leaders within the BCT is the human

resource commands assignment practices. In a perfect leader development world, company

commanders, battalion commanders, and BCT commanders would all be on the same assignment

cycle within the BCT in order to maximize the amount of time senior commanders have with

subordinates in order to train them. Professional schooling requirements, ARFORGEN, attrition,

broadening assignment opportunities, etc. all make this assignment utopia out of the question. It

is the responsibility of the BCT commander to maximize the amount of time he is assigned to the

command in developing subordinate leaders to reach their best potential and asses who will be the

leaders of the Army of tomorrow.

BCT commanders must focus on their responsibility to create an environment that

enables and supports people within the organization to learn from their experiences and those of

_____

[72] Human Resource Command Active Component Homepage, Centralized Selection List Results
Fiscal Years 10, 11, and 12, HTTPS://www.HRC.army.mil/site/active/index2.asp (Accessed 6 March,
2012)

[73] Ibid.

others.[74] This focus creates a climate of trust and learning within the BCT, capitalizing on lessons learned across the entire organization. This sharing is a form of mentorship within the BCT. It is also stressed by CSA General Casey in his guidance to commanders, "take time during reset to reflect, analyze, write down and share lessons from personal experiences with peers and subordinates."[75]

The tools available to the BCT commander in developing his subordinate commanders, mainly those at the company level, are numerous. Mentorship is but one of these tools used to ensure communication is open between the subordinate commanders and their senior commander. This is critical not only for professional development and assessment but mission accomplishment. According to his article, Caring is not enough: an Uninvited Talk to Army Leaders, LTC Harry Ingram states, "the purpose of mentoring is to provide the junior with a glimpse of the context in which the superior makes decisions."[76] This context can also aid the junior commander in understanding the senior commander's intent when directed to accomplish a task in the orders process. In order for leaders to establish this level of understanding more time together in the unit and through realistic training events is needed.

---

[74] Headquarters, U.S. Department of the Army, *FM 6-22 Army Leadership: Competent, Confident, and Agile* (Washington, D.C. 12 October 2006), 11-5.

[75] General George W. Casey Jr, *Army Training and Leader Development Guidance FY10-11* (Washington, D.C. 31 July 2009), 6.

[76] Larry H. Ingraham, "Caring is Not Enough: An Uninvited Talk to Army Leaders," *Military Review* (December 1987): 47.

"Soldiers learn to be good leaders from good leaders"[77]

-SMA Richard A. Kidd

Conclusion

History suggests that a critical element in the professional development of strategic

leaders is a superior commander who invests time and counseling in the junior officer through a

mentorship relationship. This relationship manifested differently in the four senior leaders

analyzed for this research. Generals Marshall, Bradley, Eisenhower and Patton all had someone

senior to them who took the time and effort to focus on their professional development. This

mentorship commitment was instrumental in each of them achieving incredible success in their

careers.

The amount of time each of the examples had in their assignments was strikingly

different than the career model the Army utilizes today. The years each spent in critical

developmental assignments differs dramatically with the eighteen to twenty four month time

period company commanders now spend inside a BCT. This constraint has a direct impact on the

amount of time senior commanders have to evaluate and professionally develop the subordinate

leaders, an essential part of their assignment as BCT commanders according to the field manuals

and directions of the current Army leadership.

An additional stress on the time senior leaders have with subordinate commanders is the

sheer number of company commanders that are now inside the BCT. The growth of the BCT

---

[77] Headquarters, U.S. Department of the Army, *FM 6-22 Army Leadership: Competent, Confident, and Agile* (Washington, D.C. 12 October 2006), 8-11.

from an average of fourteen company commanders in the old brigade to an average of thirty in the BCT has created a constrained amount of time a company commander's senior leader can actually spend one-on-one with them. This shortened time makes it even more important for a relationship of trust and mentorship to be established between the BCT commander and his company commanders. This relationship is crucial in everything from understanding mission command orders, commander's intent, and the desires for career progression of the junior officer when seeking advice on professional development.

Mentoring is an important tool in creating the leader that CSA Schoomaker described as a pentathelete.[78] Mentoring has many benefits for both the mentored and the senior officer. It exposes junior officers to leaders that are on average two levels up from their current position. It creates another avenue for communication to exist between senior army leaders and junior officers. This aids in addressing the concerns from the year 2000 ATLDP which are still echoed today of senior leaders out of contact with junior leaders in the Army. It aids junior leaders in a unit understand the critical elements of senior leaders guidance in everyday task and actions on the battlefield.

The battlefield in which the Army is operating today is a much more decentralized area of operations than that experienced by strategic leaders of the recent past. Training and

---

[78] SGT Sara Wood, "Soldiers Must be Adaptive for Future, Army Chief Says," *American Forces Press Service* (21 February 2006) HTTP://www.defense.gov/news/newsarticle.aspx?id=14799 (accessed 19 March 2012). Their article details the attributes of the new breed of soldier that CSA General Peter Schoomaker called the Pentathelete. He coined the term in order to describe the ability of soldiers in the future who will be able to perform a multitude of functions on the battlefield. He stated that soldiers will be required to perform other functions than their specialty skills like infantry or armor. In an interview with *Time US,* he described the pentathelete as "A whole basketball team of Michael Jordan's who can play any position. Sally B. Donnelly and Douglas Waller, "Ten Questions with Peter Schoomaker," *Time U.S.* (22 April 2005) HTTP://www.time.com/time/nation/article/0,8599,1053555,00.html (accessed 19 March 2012)

mentorship aids in bridging the experience gap junior officers have with senior leaders, even though they are required to operate in these asymmetric environments. The best way to train officers in a shortened training period on the complexities of the existing area in which they will lead is through utilization of mentorship as a tool in their professional development. This tool also allows senior officers to quickly assess junior leader's abilities as they get to know the whole person instead of a snapshot of the junior leader.

The current budgetary constraint on the Army are forcing it to dramatically cut force structure. These cuts are reducing the number of BCT's. This reduction could have an impact on the ARFORGEN management model and affect the amount of time leaders have on professional development and training at home station, both which are critical in the development of the future strategic leaders.

In an attempt to address the concerns of the lack of boots on the ground in the current BCTs, one of the proposals that Army leadership is looking at is creating another maneuver battalion inside the BCT. This additional battalion of soldiers would greatly increase the overall effectiveness of the BCT in the current counter insurgency conflict in Afghanistan and, perceivably, the most likely combat scenarios of the future. One of the second or third order effects of adding this additional battalion is the impact on the overall development of the junior leaders within these BCTs. The amount of time the senior commander will have with all of the company commanders will be substantially reduced again by the addition of the maneuver company commanders in the new battalion. According to Kathy Kram, the most important element in the mentoring relationship is time that the leader has with the mentored and this will be directly impacted by the growth of the BCT.[79]

Forcing mentorship to be used as a developmental tool within the Army could have adverse effects on the overall effectiveness of it. The mentor and the mentee must sincerely desire the relationship to exist for it to be an effective tool. Making it mandatory will most likely lead mentoring to be another block check in the professional development process instead of a mutually beneficial relationship that produces the type of leadership displayed by Eisenhower or Bradley. Instead, the Army should continue to stress the advantages that mentorship offers to the tool kit of the BCT commander and provide more examples of successful mentorship experiences within its own literature. The example of Fox Conner and Eisenhower, placed inside of the leadership manuals, would go a long way to reinforcing the importance mentorship has in not only the Army's historical reference but as an example of how to grow the strategic leaders of the future.

The proposal to increase the BCT by an additional maneuver battalion will provide the much needed increase in maneuver forces within the BCT in the current counter insurgency fight. The additional maneuver battalion will increase the lethality and span of influence of a BCT in wide area security and combined arms maneuver during a conventional operation. The RSTA battalion could then focus on its core mission task of finding the enemy in a conventional fight for the BCT commander and enabling the maneuver battalions to finish the enemy decisively.

---

[79] Kathy E Kram, *Mentoring at Work: Developmental Relationships in Organizational Life* (Boston, MA: University Press of America, 1988), 19.

44

In order to address the time issue the current BCT commander faces while training and developing his company commanders, the Army should increase the time leaders are in units together. Changing the current command policy from two year to three year tours at company through BCT level will increase the time senior leaders have to be involved in junior leader development through multiple training events or deployments. This would also coincide with the new ARFORGEN model of one year deployment to two years at home station.

These recommendations would take little time to initiate within the Army. The biggest impact would be on the amount of officer backlog for key and developmental positions, such as command. This backlog would be alleviated in the long run by creating more time between command positions therefore allowing more officers to attend career broadening assignments that are being espoused by senior leaders today.

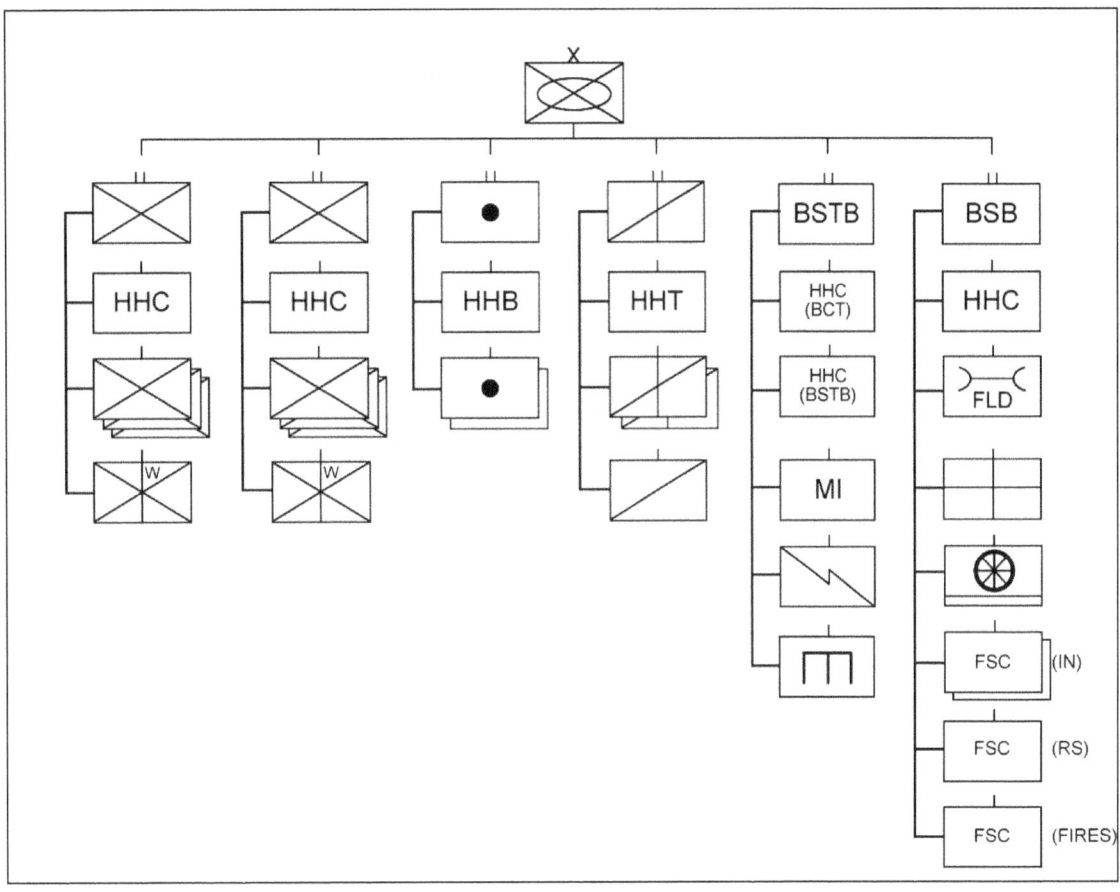

Infantry Brigade Combat Team[80]

---

[80] Headquarters, U.S. Department of the Army, *FM 3-90.6 Brigade Combat Team* (Washington, D.C. September 2010), 1-10.

APPENDIX 2

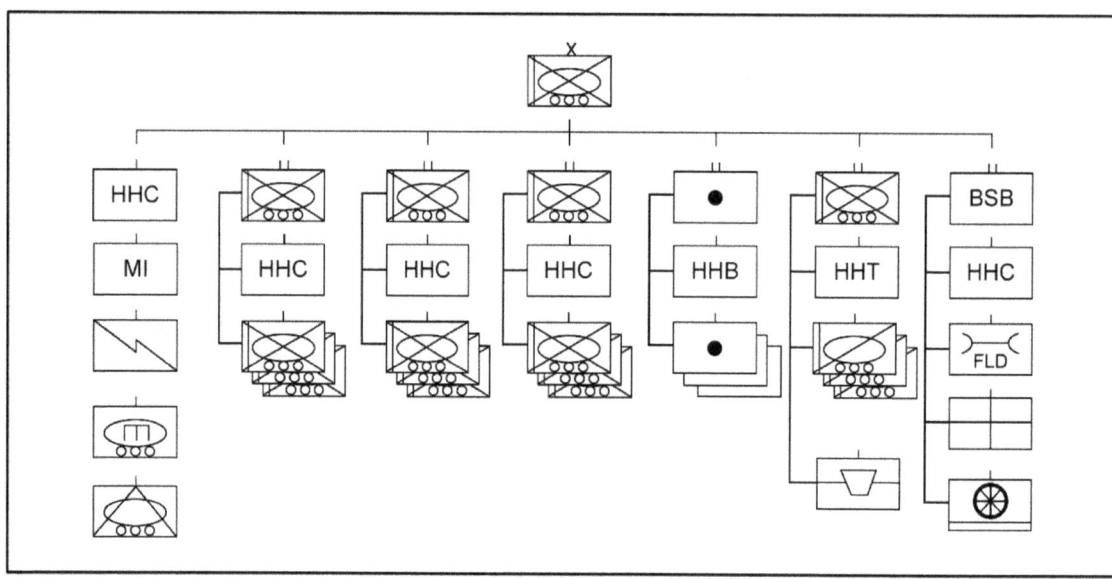

Heavy Brigade Combat Team[81]

---

[81] Headquarters, U.S. Department of the Army, *FM 3-90.6 Brigade Combat Team* (Washington, D.C. September 2010), 1-7.

APPENDIX 3

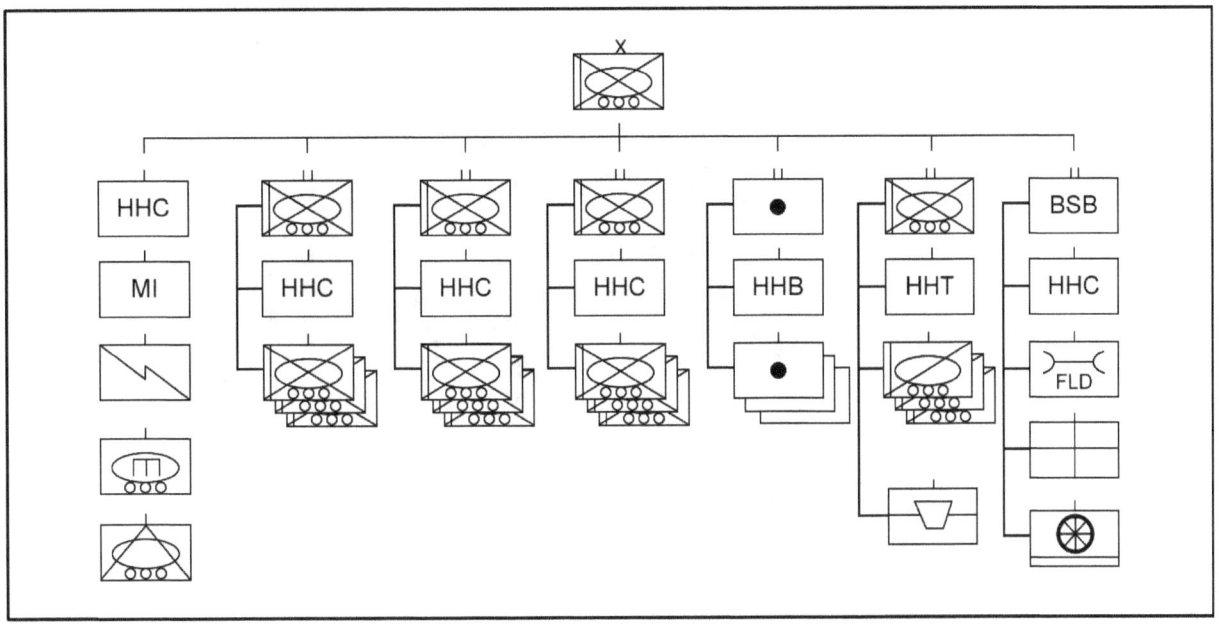

Stryker Brigade Combat Team[82]

---

[82] Headquarters, U.S. Department of the Army, *FM 3-90.6 Brigade Combat Team* (Washington, D.C. September 2010), 1-13.

APPENDIX 4

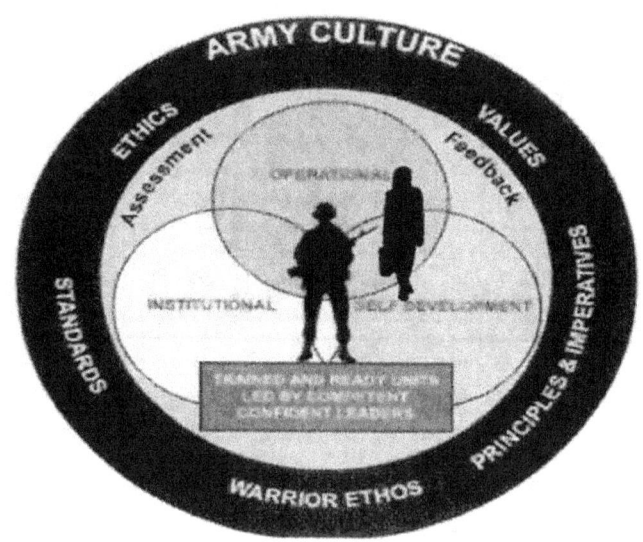

The Army Training and Leader Development Model[83]

This model derived from Army Regulation 350-1, Army Training and Leader

Development , depicts the interaction among three separate but overlapping domains (operational,

institutional and self-development) that must be synchronized in order to achieve the goal of

trained Soldiers, Army civilians, leaders, and ready units.[84]

---

[83] Headquarters, U.S. Department of the Army, *AR 350-1 Army Training and Leader Development* (Washington, D.C. December 2009), 4.

[84] Ibid.

APPENDIX 5

	Leads Others	Extends Influence Beyond the Chain of Command	Leads by Example	Communicates
Leads	• Provide purpose, motivation, inspiration. • Enforce standards. • Balance mission and welfare of Soldiers.	• Build trust outside lines of authority. • Understand sphere, means, and limits of influence. • Negotiate, build consensus, resolve conflict.	• Display character. • Lead with confidence in adverse conditions. • Demonstrate competence.	• Listen actively. • State goals for action. • Ensure shared understanding.
	Creates a Positive Environment	Prepares Self	Develops Leaders	
Develops	• Set the conditions for positive climate. • Build teamwork and cohesion. • Encourage initiative. • Demonstrate care for people.	• Be prepared for expected and unexpected challenges. • Expand knowledge. • Maintain self-awareness.	• Assess developmental needs. Develop on the job. • Support professional and personal growth. • Help people learn. • Counsel, coach, and mentor. • Build team skills and processes.	
	Gets Results			
Achieves	• Provide direction, guidance, and priorities. • Develop and execute plans. • Accomplish tasks consistently.			

Eight core leader competencies and supporting behaviors[85]

---

[85] Headquarters, U.S. Department of the Army, *FM 6-22 Army Leadership: Competent, Confident, and Agile* (Washington, D.C. 12 October 2006), 2-7.

50

APPENDIX 6

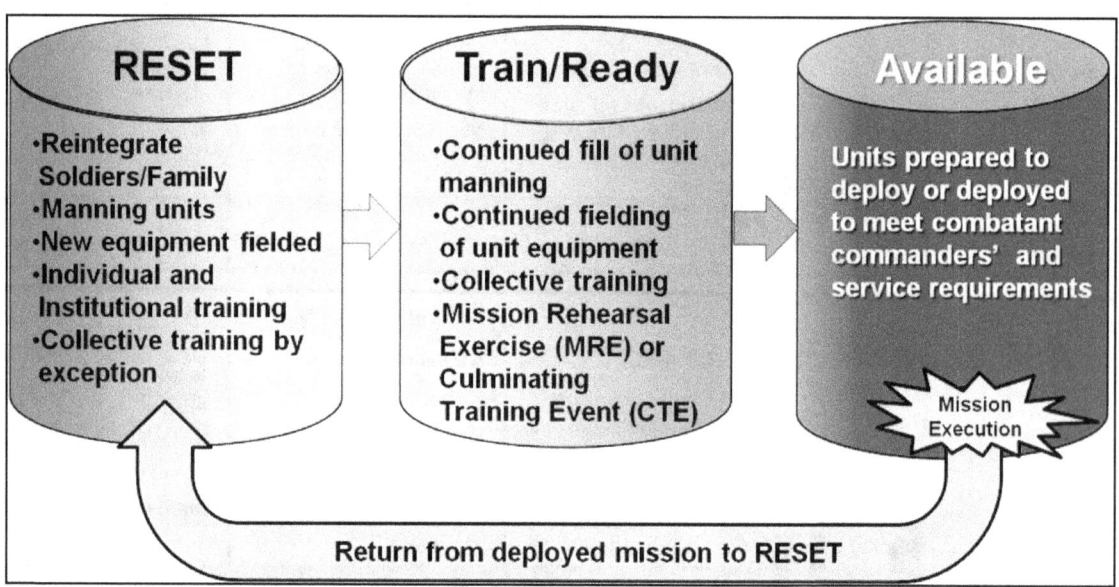

Army Force Generation Model [86]

---

[86] General J.D.Thurman, Infantry Warfighting Conference Brief (Atlanta, Georgia: U.S. Army Forces Command, 14 September 2010)

BIBLIOGRAPHY

Ambrose, Stephen E. *Ike/Abilene to Berlin,* New York: Harper and Row Publishers, 1973.

Bacon, Lance M. "Army to Lose another 5 BCTs," *Army Times* (March 5, 2012)

Bagnal, Charles W, Earle C. Pence, and Thomas N. Meriwether. "Leaders as Mentors." *Military Review*, (July 1985): 4-20.

Bodner, Diana L. *The Relationship between Fox Conner and Dwight Eisenhower.* Strategy Research Project, Carlisle Barracks, PA: U.S. Army War College, 2002.

Bradley, Omar, N. and Clay Blair, *A General's Life.* New York: Simon and Schuster, 1983.

Cabrey, Richard M, Mark E McKnight, and David S Cannon. "The Marshall Approach: The Battle Command Training Program and the 21st-century Leader Development." *Military Review,* (March-April 2010): 98-101.

Camacho, Lawrence F. *The Leadership Development of Dwight D. Eisenhower and George S Patton JR.* SAMS Monograph, Fort Leavenworth, School of Advanced Military Studies, 2009.

Casey, George W. Jr, General. *Army Training and Leader Development Guidance FY10-11.* Washington, D.C. 31 July 2009.

Cohen, Eliot A. *Supreme Command.* New York: Free Press, 2002.

D'Este, Carlo. *Patton: A Genius for War.* New York: HarperCollins Publishers, 1995.

Donnelly, Sally B. and Douglas Waller. "Ten Questions with Peter Schoomaker." *Time U.S.* (22 April 2005) HTTP://www.time.com/time/nation/article/0,8599,1053555,00.html (accessed 19 March 2012)

Dooley, Joseph C. *George C Marshall: A study in mentorship.* USAWC Military Studies Program Paper. An Individual Study Project, Carlisle Barracks, PA: U.S. Army War College, 1990.

Dreazon, Yochi J. "U.S. Strategy in Afghan War Hinges on Far-Flung Outpost." *The Wall Street Journal* (4 Mar 2009) HTTP://www.online.wsj.com/article/SB12361181947423107.html (accessed 19 March 2012).

Eisenhower, Dwight D. *At Ease: Stories I Tell to Friends.* Garden City, *New* York: Doubleday and Company, 1967.

Everly, D.R. *U.S. Army Captains: Unprepared for Tomorrow's Challenges.* Quantico, VA: United States Marine Corps Command and Staff College, 2008.

Franks, Tommy. *American Soldier.* New York: Regan Books, 2004.

Feickert, Andrew. *U.S. Army's Modular Redesign: Issues for Congress.* Congressional Research Service, Library of Congress. Washington D.C. 5 May, 2006:14.

Hale, Mathew T. *Mentoring Junior Leaders: Leadership Tools for our 21st Century Army.* Strategy Research Project, Carlisle Barracks, PA: U.S. Army War College, 2001.

Headquarters, Department of the Army. *United States Army White Paper: Concepts for the Objective Force.* Washington, DC, June 2001.

Headquarters, Department of the Army. *Field Manual 6-22: Army Leadership.* Washington, DC, 12 October 2006.

Headquarters, Department of the Army Training and Doctrine Command. *TRADOC Pam 525-3-0: The Army Capstone Concept.* Fort Monroe, VA, 21 December 2009.

Headquarters, Department of the Army Training and Doctrine Command. *TRADOC Pam 350-10: Institutional Leader Training And Education.* Fort Monroe, VA, 12 August 2002.

Headquarters, Department of the Army Training and Doctrine Command. *TRADOC Pam 525-3-1: The United States Army Operating Concept.* Fort Monroe, VA, 19 August 2010.

Headquarters, Department of the Army. Field Manual 3-21.21: The Stryker Brigade Combat Team Infantry Battalion. Washington, DC, April 2003.

Headquarters, Department of the Army. *Field Manual 3-90.6: Brigade Combat Team.* Washington, DC, September 2010.

Headquarters, Department of the Army. *Army Mentorship Handbook .* Rosslyn, VA, 2005. http://www.armycounselingonline.com/downloads/army-mentorship-handbook/

Headquarters, U.S. Department of the Army, *At a Strategic Crossroads: 2011 Army Posture Statement.* Washington, D.C. March 2011.

Headquarters, U.S. Department of the Army, *2010 U.S. Army Posture Statement.* Washington, D.C. 1 December 2009. HTTPS://secureweb2.hqda.pentagon.mil/vdas_armyposturestatement/2010/information_papers_combate_training_center_CTC_program.asp (Accessed 20 March 2012)

Headquarters, U.S. Department of the Army, *FM 3-24 Counterinsurgency.* Washington, D.C. December 2006.

Headquarters, U.S. Department of the Army, *AR 350-1 Army Training and Leader Development.* Washington, D.C. December 2009.

Herspring, Dale R. *The Pentagon and the Presidency.* Lawrence, KS: University Press of Kansas, 2005.

Hirai, James T and Kim L Summers. "Leader Development and Education: Growing Leaders Now for the Future." *Military Review*, (May-June 2005): 86-95.

Horner, Donald H. "Leader Development and Why It Remains Important." *Military Review*, (July-August 1995): 76-87.

Human Resource Command Active Component Homepage, Centralized Selection List Results Fiscal year 10, 11, and 12. HTTPS://www.HRC.army.mil/site/active/index2.asp (Accessed 6 March, 2012)

Hunsinger, Nate. "Mentorship: Growing Company Grade Officers," *Military Review,* (September-October 2004): 82.

Huntington, Samuel P. *The Soldier and the State.* Cambridge: Belknap Press of Harvard University Press, 1957.

Ingraham, Larry H. "Caring is Not Enough: An Uninvited Talk To Army Leaders." *Military Review,* (December 1987): 45-48.

Kingseed, Cole C. "Mentoring General Ike." *Military Review,* (October 1990): 26-30.

Kraft, Nelson G. *The Infantry Brigade Combat Team: The U.S. Army's Premier Phase IV and Irregular Warfare Force for the 21st Century* Maxwell AFB, AL: Air University, Air Command and Staff College, 2007.

Kram, Kathy E. *Mentoring at Work: Developmental Relationships in Organizational Life.* Boston, MA: University Press of America, 1988.

Krepinevich, Andrew F. *Strategy for the Long Haul: An Army at the Crossroads.* Washington D.C. Center for Strategic and Budgetary Assessments, 2008.

Kopser, G. Joseph. "Mentoring in the Military: Not Everybody Gets It," *Military Review* (November-December 2002): 40.

Lambeth, Benjamen S. "Task Force Hawk." *Air Force Magazine,* (February 2002): 83.

Leed, Maren and David Sokolow. *The Ingenuity Gap: Officer Management for the 21st Century.* Washington D.C.: Center for Strategic and International Studies, 2010.

Lewis, James M. *Trust and Dialogue in the Army Profession.* SAMS Monograph, Fort Leavenworth, School of Advanced Military Studies, 2008.

Livingston, Russell M. *Reality vs. Myth: Mentoring Reexamined.* SAMS Monograph, Fort Leavenworth, School of Advanced Military Studies, 2010.

Maggart, Lon E and Jeanette S James. "Mentoring-A Critical Element in Leader Development." *Military Review,* (May-June 1999): 86-87.

Magee, Roderick R. "Building Strategic Leadership for the 21st Century." *Military Review,* (February 1993): 36-44.

Martin, Theodore D. *Developing Strategic Leaders for the War After Next.* Strategy Research Project, Carlisle Barracks, PA: U.S. Army War College, 2007.

Margotta, Mathew T. *Creating the "Pentathelete:" Are we willing to pay the price?* Carlisle Barracks, PA: Civilian Research Project, U.S. Army War College, 2007.

Melanson, Mark A. "The Mentoring Spectrum." *The Army Medical Department Journal* (October-December 2009): 37-39. HTTP://www.cs.amedd.army.mil/dasqaDocuments.aspx?type=1. (Accessed 28 December 2011)

Melanson, Mark A. "Leadership Wisdom." *The Army Medical Department Journal* (October-December 2009): 17-20. HTTP://www.cs.amedd.army.mil/dasqaDocuments.aspx?type=1. (Accessed 28 December 2011)

Melanson, Mark A. "Seasons of Army Mentorship and the Mentoring Staircase." *The Army Medical Department Journal* (October-December 2009): 40-43. HTTP://www.cs.amedd.army.mil/dasqaDocuments.aspx?type=1. (Accessed 28 December 2011)

Mentor Quotes, http://www.self-improvement-mentor.com/famous-leadership-quotes.html (Accessed 29 December, 2011)

Moss, Francis R. *The Costs and Benefits of Adding a Third Maneuver Battalion to the Brigade Combat Team.* SAMS Monograph, Fort Leavenworth, School of Advanced Military Studies, 2008.

Munoz, Carlo. "Army Eyes Deeper Brigade Combat Team Cuts, Odierno Says," *AoL Defense.* (24 February 2012), HTTP://www.defemse.aol.com/2012/02/24/army-eyes-deeper-brigade-combat-team-cuts-odierno-says (accessed 12 March 2012).

Pierce, William G. *Span of Control and the Operational Commander: Is it More Than Just a Number?* SAMS Monograph, Fort Leavenworth, School of Advanced Military Studies, 1991.

Poque, Forrest C. *George C. Marshall: Education of a General 1880-1939.* New York: The Viking Press, 1963.

Rocke, Mark D.Major and Major Thomas W. Hayden, "Officer Development: A Doctrinal Imperative," *Military Review* (January 1993): 29.

Rumsfeld, Donald. *Known and Unknown: A memoir.* New York: New York: Penguin books, 2011.

Ruvolo, Catherine M, Scott A. Peterson, and Joseph N.G. LeBoeuf. "Leaders Are Made, Not Born: The critical role of a developmental framework to facilitate an organizational culture of development." *Consulting Psychology Journal: Practice and Research* (Winter 2004):10-19.

Sandoy, Andrew S. *Span of Control Initiatives: Is more, Less?* SAMS Monograph, Fort Leavenworth, School of Advanced Military Studies, 1990.

Schoomaker, Peter General and Major Anthony Vassalo, "The Way Ahead," *Military Review* (March-April 2004): 5.

Steele, William M. Lieutenant General and Lieutenant Colonel Robert P. Walters. "Training and Developing Army Leaders." *Military Review* (July-August 2001): 4.

Steinberg, Alma G. and Susann M. Nourizadeh. *Superior, Peer, and Subordinate Mentoring in the U.S. Army.* Alexandria, VA: U.S. Army Research Institute, 2001.

Tan, Michael. "Staying tough on standards," *Army Times* (December 5, 2011)

Thurman, J.D. General. *Infantry Warfighting Conference Brief.* Atlanta, Georgia: U.S. Army Forces Command, 14 September 2010.

Tichy, Noel and Eli Cohen. *The Leadership Engine: How Winning Companies Build Leaders at Every Level.* New York, New York: Harper Collins Publishing, 1997.

Turabian, Kate L. *A Manual for Writers of Research Papers, Theses, and Dissertations.* 7th ed. Chicago: University of Chicago Press, 2007.

U.S. Congress. Congressional Budget Office. *Options for Restructuring the Army.* House Committee on Armed Service, Washington, DC, May 2005.

Vanden Brook, Tom. "Defense Secretary Leon Panetta defends a leaner military," *USA Today* (January 1, 2012), HTTP://www.usatoday.com/news/washington/story/2012-01-26/panetta-military-defense-cuts/52805056/1 (accessed 12 March 2012).

Washington, Bette R. *"Mentorship: An Army Dilemma."* Strategy Research Project, Carlisle Barracks, PA: U.S. Army War College, 2002.

Wass de Czege, Huba and Richard Hart Sinnreich, *Conceptual Foundations of a Transformed US Army.* Washington, DC: Institute for Land Warfare, March 2002.

Whiteside, Craig. "From One to Three Sixty: Assessing Leaders." *Military Review,* (September-October 2004): 86-88.

Wood, Sara. SGT. "Soldiers Must be Adaptive for Future, Army Chief Says," *American Forces Press Service* (21 February 2006) HTTP://www.defense.gov/news/newsarticle.aspx?id=14799 (accessed 19 March 2012).